Theodore Deppe

LIMINAL BLUE

ARLEN HOUSE

Liminal Blue

is published in 2016 by

ARLEN HOUSE
42 Grange Abbey Road
Baldoyle
Dublin 13
Ireland
Phone/Fax: 353 86 8207617
Email: arlenhouse@gmail.com
arlenhouse.blogspot.com

Distributed internationally by
SYRACUSE UNIVERSITY PRESS
621 Skytop Road, Suite 110
Syracuse, NY 13244–5290
Phone: 315–443–5534/Fax: 315–443–5545
Email: supress@syr.edu

978–1–85132–134–6, paperback

Typesetting by Arlen House

Cover image 'Liminal Blue' by Caitlin Deppe

Liminal Blue

Contents

for Theodore Deppe
1921–2013

Alice Minot Deppe
1924–2009

and, as always, for Annie

LIMINAL BLUE

I

Vertigo and Adagio

That particular part of the trip – the journey's
beginning – I hadn't figured out. Large hills
terrified me and the train was climbing
the north slopes of the Alps. I was nineteen
and as night drew near I feared another attack
like those I'd had all year, brief moments
when my mind jolted an inch or two above
and behind my head. So far, they'd passed, but if
they were portents of something larger …?
A glance out the window (the winter moon
tinted the snow a dangerous shade of blue),
then, for distraction, memorising Rilke. *Beauty*
is nothing but the beginning of terror
we are just able to bear. Far below, village lights
like a broken string of beads, and the headlights
of a lone car inching up a mountain road
towards a second hamlet, itself suspended in night.
Then a tunnel – abrupt as an attack – and my book
dropped, I braced myself and listened
to the rhythm of wheels, practised breathing.
The train emerged above a higher valley,
skirted the precipice, kept climbing.

At last it happened: I didn't have to avert my eyes.
Somehow I found courage to watch,
and by morning the snowbound heights
gave way to plum orchards
blossoming in the Italian foothills. My journal says
that up there in that wild night I started humming
the adagio movement of Beethoven's
String Quartet in A minor, that sublime work I'd heard
a month earlier. I'd sat in the concert hall, fearing
if I let myself go too far into beauty
I might trigger the next assault. I'd never felt

so foolish in my life – I was six-foot-one
and about to be destroyed by a piece of music.
My hands gripped the seat, but why go on living
if I couldn't listen? I'm grateful now
to that boy who closed his eyes,
gave himself over to all that followed.

A Nap on Inis Meáin

Not the ruins of Inis Meáin's churches or forts
or the cottage where Synge stayed
or the rocky chair where he wrote for hours

but comforters for a nap among blackbird songs
and the call of summer's first cuckoo.
After journeying through mountains and bogs,

after crossing choppy Galway Bay,
there's just time to travel a few sentences
in a new book before closing your eyes

with fog at the window, the sounds of Irish
in the kitchen and the whole dream island
stretching before you.

Meet me, if you can, in the lane
above Gregory's Sound, at this blue gate
in a stone wall. While you are sleeping,

I've walked through moving sheets
of light mist and made it as far
as this bright colour.

A gate this blue must exist in both
the sleeping and the waking world.
Waves make a golden thunder

on the shore below and a skylark
sings above. Meet me, if you can,
at the gate of the marvellous on Inis Meáin.

Primary

Forty-eight years since I joined
a bus of college students to Milwaukee
and walked door to door, handing out leaflets,
wishing the campaign organisers
had taught us a few phrases of Polish,

but it didn't matter, I smiled and repeated
Eugene McCarthy, please vote
for Eugene McCarthy,
as snow showers began, my hands
started shaking and I wondered

how many of these immigrants
were citizens yet and whether
a single mind was being changed.
One face stays with me –
called from Sunday dinner, a man

tried hard to understand
what I was saying, as if knowing
why I was there might be important,
important but impossible,
an old man, large nose, intense eyes,

a face like a late Rembrandt self-portrait,
and everything I said – *Vietnam, primary,*
urgent, peace – made him
shake his head sorrowfully, speak to me
in Polish and finally take his leave.

Then we were back on the bus to Indiana,
night came on, the highway
flew past glacier-flattened fields
and our leader stood up
and repeated the radio's news.

Lyndon Johnson had withdrawn from the race
and the bus seemed to lift a bit above the road.
The anti-war movement was winning!
Of course, what we got in the end
was Nixon and seven more years of war.

How I'd love to be on that bus again,
everyone for some reason singing *Lady Madonna,*
Route 65 leading us south through the night,
believing real progress possible, tasting
it. What did the man with Rembrandt's face

understand of my words? And
what couldn't he say to me? Poland at the time
was part of a Soviet Union
that seemed impossible to change, so having lived
history, having witnessed

what it could do to those he loved,
what did he make of this teenager at his door?
And here I am, probably older now than he was then,
with no good answers to the questions
I thought I read in his eyes.

I liked that he seemed to want
to understand me. That he kept smiling,
however ruefully, at a stranger. That he accepted
the leaflet he probably couldn't read.
That he shut the door gently.

For the Time Being

Oh strange party of the heart. Who
in that living room was what we call alive?
Mother was newly-dead of course, that's why

her friend Laura invited us to her Derby party,
Laura who said, *Alice's obituary is*
perfect, except for one word – you described

your parents' wartime romance as a whirlwind,
but your mother told me their courtship was
torrid. Strange heartfelt party

where somnambulists who felt like weeping
instead placed bets
on which horse might blaze fastest.

In post-war Paris, Laura passed a gallery
each evening and longed for the Modigliani
in the window. One bereft day it was gone.

Then finding it was only being cleaned, she gambled
everything and made an offer. Modigliani,
the spectacular, the impossible

man, who had tuberculosis by sixteen and knew
his only chance was *a brief but intense life.*
And out of the wreckage he made

of that knowledge, out of absinthe,
out of poverty, out of hashish,
out of treating those he loved

terribly, came this serene portrait,
a young Polish émigré,
head at a slight tilt,

nose long and curving as an Orthodox Madonna's,
piled-up dark hair just beginning to unravel
above a small, colourful smile. *Sixty-three years*

she's travelled with me, Laura told my father.
Almost as long as you and Alice were married.
Laura's gone now, the painting is journeying

someplace new, and I'm told
that Laura's friend at the party, Hana,
has also died. Hearing Hana was from Prague,

Dad said, *Lovely city! I was there once,*
then stopped himself, realising
it wasn't part of his grand tour – he'd seen it

from the air, seen it beneath flak and flames.
So many ghosts, especially at parties.
Under the Polish woman's portrait, the sweet taste

of strong mint juleps, Mother
at the centre of things, my father smiling
on the edge of tears as the horses burst

from their floodgates, colours surging
above a wet-fast track,
all of us hovering between a hush and a shout,

and it was the horse so far back its jockey couldn't see
the rest of the field, the 50–to–1 gelding
that charged the rail so quickly the announcer

missed him till he was clear –
a spectacular upset, an impossible
result! Mother, after twelve days of sleepwalking

we woke to find ourselves applauding
a jockey with a Cajun accent
who tossed a rose to the sky, the son who left school

after ninth grade but promised his parents
he would amount to something,
and in this party going on in my heart

where some of us were dead and the rest
must follow soon enough
everyone for the time

being was singing, and the words went
Weep no more, my lady.
None of us picked the winner, but we cheered

the horse from nowhere,
we threw our brief, intense roses
into the waiting air.

October Postcards from Connemara

One day I will answer. One day when I am dead and can at last concentrate. Or at least so far away from here that I can find myself again.
– Tomas Tranströmer, 'Answers to Letters'

Beaufort wind scale, Force 9: Back from Stockholm before the weather. In the bright field across the lane, south winds collide with the west's strong gale and tall grasses eddy and whirl. I walk out to stand in that flux and reel, let the gusts stagger me and remember your crossing to a house during an Icelandic hurricane, feeling like you were drowning on dry land.

Force 6: I'd meant to write while you were still alive. Sunday, we followed your memoir through the streets of Södermalm and found the divorce flat where you moved with your mother. Two women entered the tenement and we caught the door before it closed and locked. A plaque inside with a poem that records the nightmares you experienced there. Riding the tiny elevator to the top floor, where you waited out the night, I felt anxious and at home.

Force 8: I loved your description of being an extra in the film Ingmar Bergman shot at your grammar school and how he captured the mood of the place. Across the bay, waves strike the cliffs on Caher Island, then hang in the air ten seconds. Twelve. Fifteen.

Force 10: Eyes keep watering, so who knows what I'm seeing! On the road, rainwater runs uphill like reversed cascades. White fireworks all along the cliffs, celebrating the beginning or the end of things. I expect to see signposts for the Wild Atlantic Way turned into projectiles. Mark the Post arrives in his green-and-white van, says, *It's bad, okay, but even worse up the coast.* I imagine giving him this postcard for you and his taking it like a sacred trust, disappearing down our lane, carrying news from this world into the blast.

Force 1: And then the storm is gone, like a man who thinks when he's finished shouting the whole world can start to calm. Walking to the cove, I think of the lovesick Tibetan monk who gave thanks for swimming, because, for many of us, it was the only time our bare feet ever touch earth, sand or sea. Mother used to call wind the Holy Spirit. But reports say the storm forming in the Caribbean would be the world's twentieth-largest country, if storms could be nations.

Force 0: The Kingdom of the Midges. Take shelter in a strong pub.

Force 2: Tomas, we boarded a ferry bound for the Baltics, wanting to see the labyrinth your ship pilot grandfather could negotiate in thick fog, as if he had memorised the whole maze. How wonderful, to have been a boy with a very good friend who was seventy-one years older than you. A grandfather who could read the invisible. I wish I could see just a little ahead, could help our children navigate what comes next.

Force 5: Rain, of course, comes next. Waves race across a lake where the meadow used to be.

Force 7: In your sequence, 'Baltics', you imagined a composer who suffered a stroke. Paralysed on the right side, robbed of most words, he composes in his own style with his left hand. Fifteen years later, you suffered just such a brain haemorrhage and taught yourself to play piano with your left hand. Listening to your music, I keep increasing the volume as wind ratchets up its din.

Force 9: Snot from my nostrils sails a hundred metres over the bracken. The bellowing of our neighbour's bull flies by. The sound of the sea drawing rocks down the shingle and hurling them back. Night, now, and this whistling and banging at the windows must be like what Beethoven began hearing in his 28th year, forcing him early on to become an exile, to become a philosopher.

Force 11: A thumping in the stove as wind feeds on flames almost as fast as I can fuel the fire. Only one more level left on the wind scale but already there are symphonic howls all around me. I put on headphones and play your recording: sounds struck so softly they glisten almost visibly. When my turn comes to die, might I listen to this music again and follow your left hand along the keys, note by note, through the archipelago, out to the open sea.

In a Hill Town I Didn't Enter when I was Nineteen

Il Giorno dei Morti, my sixtieth birthday –
we're the only visitors in this one-painting museum

where two angels part the curtain
and a young peasant opens her dress

with the gravitas and grace of a pregnant queen.
Mother, where else should I have come,

now you are gone? The angels' wings
are green, rust and gold, the colours

of November vineyards in Monterchi
where the artist's mother was born; here, too,

she is buried, and he painted
the *Madonna del Parto*

for the cemetery chapel. Birth and death
in the same embroidered tent, the grave

and the gravid girl. The slight downturn
of the Virgin's lips, sorrowful, sublime.

I stand still so long the lights flick off.
So much death, but once, in such darkness,

they say love curled up and took form.
Alone in this room, I don't know how to pray,

I keep repeating my thanks
and the walls won't stop shaking.

Say it was Just Jet Lag

Waking after walking through bombed-out Dresden
I was grateful to find no charred corpses in our bedroom,
no collapsed buildings,
though I knew that meant the ruins must be inside me.

Say it was just jet lag, the eight time zones
from San Francisco to Ireland impeding sleep,
but the images of those burned streets
reappeared each time I closed my eyes.

Up, then, trying to reclaim myself
from the rubble of the unconscious;
I brushed my hair, put on a clean shirt,
as if that would make me presentable,

then looked up Richard Peter's famous
soulscape of Dresden, taken
after climbing many stairs to nowhere.
Finally, he willed

a ladder up the City Hall's damaged tower steps
and took his photograph over the shoulder
of the statue of *Gute,* of Goodness, as she stretched
her hands out over six square miles of destruction.

Somewhere down there
is where I was walking.
But in Dresden's filigreed fragments, in all those
skeletal realms, I can't see a single living thing.

~

Dresden, again. Three sleep-challenged nights in,
I seem to have come unstuck in time,

like Kurt Vonnegut's Billy Pilgrim, and was startled
to relive an instant from five years ago

when, after climbing the long steps
from the sub-basement of Slaughterhouse-Five,
Annie and I paused with the German schoolteacher
who was Virgiling us

and I was uncertain when the iron door opened
whether I'd see Dresden as it was then, in 2011,
or as it was on Ash Wednesday, 1941,
when prisoners emerged with their guards

under a pinprick sun in the black clouds of noon
and witnessed what mile-high
tornadoes of fire had done.
Did Vonnegut know before he died that this place

is now a party space? Concert hall or no,
this building keeps flipping back
to being a slaughterhouse and then a prison
and its door still opens onto the unspeakable.

~

That night, after touring Slaughterhouse-Five,
I almost wrote a poem for Vonnegut,
addressing him as if from that moment at the threshold
where worlds seemed to overlap,

but elegies are often just letters
we waited too long to write
and I had missed my chance to talk with him.
In 2000, our lives overlapped for a few weeks

in Northampton. His seemed haunted
by flames: he'd rented a couple of rooms
from our good friend Kerry, after leaving New York
where a Pall Mall set fire to his wastebasket.

~

We followed Vonnegut's footsteps
into a city still being rebuilt
sixty-six years later, and it seemed
that Beautiful Dresden

was as achronological as a dream.
Like a magician who lets the audience in on her trick,
she pointed to the spot where the flow
of a graceful Baroque street

was interrupted by a metal crane,
hovering above scaffolding,
as antique windows were fitted to facades
and the past was painstakingly restored.

~

How does one ever sleep again after witnessing
so much death – did 20,000 die, or was it 120,000,
as Vonnegut believed? No one knows: so many
were simply vaporised and could not be counted.

Even just one death – how did he
give himself to the night
after his mother's suicide
during his visit on Mother's Day?

We take our nightmare collections
with us wherever we go,
the little shrines we cover with black drapes
and try not to stare at.

~

No. Some artists are able to look at those images
for the time it takes to testify. Richard Peter,
returning to find his home in ruins, refused
to look away and composed his book of witness.

And Vonnegut spent a lifetime bringing night terrors
to the page, leavening them with hospital humour.
Which doesn't mean he wasn't frightened.
Not long before his death, Vonnegut called from New York

and asked his former landlady
to sing him something before bed.
Kerry is a woman who can sing the blues
and she treated him to 'I'm going to love you

like nobody's loved you,
come rain or come shine'.
He was eighty-four and marking off the days –
didn't he claim he would sue

the cigarette company that had promised
their product would end him,
but after seven decades of chain-smoking Pall Malls
he was still alive, killing time –

but that doesn't make it easier to face the dark alone.
It must have felt like Goodness herself, a woman
reaching out to him on the phone with a song.
'Happy together, unhappy together, and won't it be fine'.

THE DREAM OF HOME

Riding down from mountain snow,
the horse-drawn cart, blankets about me
like a wool cocoon, night,

and we enter a hamlet, horseshoes chiming
in the still-sleeping streets, and below us, the lights
of another village, we keep descending,

always another lower cluster of lights,
then somehow daybreak, winter in the heights
but spring begins now

with slant sun and plum blossoms and look,
my childhood home from Indiana, how did it
come to be in these foothills, and how wonderful

that the horse stops, I can walk again in the old yard,
the apple tree I thought had died
blooms like water straight from the source,

and I would stay here longer if it were possible,
explore the house and find where the singing
comes from, but it's time to return to the mountain,

the horse starts off at a brisk pace,
out of the remembered, back to the drifts
that cover everything, starlit snowfields,

hoof beats muffled in the spinning heights,
as it was in the beginning, as it was in the time
before there was time, before there were homes.

A Field Near the Seine

Georges Braque, *The Shower*, oil on canvas, 1952

Two world wars in his garden and what he goes back now to paint is that field in 1900. Almost seventy and his morning leads back past the battle for Normandy, back past Picasso, the conflicts and the time they were roped together like mountain climbers, taking peaks apart and remaking them, finding footholds where they could reinvent the world, back past 1915 and the shrapnel that blinded him for days, and back finally to that meadow by the Seine where one century was ending and a new one bursting upon him. He might have cycled right by, but a flat tyre forced him to stop and see that wheat field, a meadow of waving grain miles from anything he knew, his parents a day behind in Le Havre and the Montparnasse rooms he would live in next still something he had to imagine, so for those few hours he was more alone than he had ever been, without a repair kit as rain approached. So why did he feel so at home? More than half a century later, he paints that field over and over. Eventually, he stuffed wheat into the tyre, a memorably sorry solution, but he was eighteen, bicycling to Paris, and if he couldn't say what that field meant to him, he could try to paint it, a daub of pink on the bark of one of the trees, then plum, then blue, letting cubism go for now, painting the place the way his teenaged self might have. After the horrors he'd witnessed, why not keep creating still lifes with skulls and the plates with two black fish? But something about that meadow resists explanation, so he dabs a touch of mulberry to the tree that shelters the wounded bicycle, then starts in on the sunlit shower, silvery slashes that once approached and briefly surrounded him and made the scene of his bike's breakdown glisten.

By Now Our Lives Should Have Crossed

> Somewhere sometime we must have
> passed one another like going and coming trains,
> with both of us looking the other way.
> – Lisel Mueller, 'Palindrome', *Alive Together*

It's 3 at night in the Kreuzberg flat we sublet
from friends and I'm looking through Eva's library,

I'm whispering, *Ask, and it shall be given you,*
words that may be the Lord's

but it was my mother's voice tonight
that spoke them and woke me –

Seek, and ye shall find, and the book
my hand discovers is written by a woman

born on 8 February 1924. The same day
as my mother. From Germany, where she says

her family's bookshelves *connected heaven and earth,*
I follow Lisel Mueller to the American Midwest

and find that in 1953 she and my mother
lived in the same town. 1953, the year

Mueller's mother died, the year she began writing
because, she said, the world went on

blossoming, and language was *the only thing*
that would grieve with me. Now, my mother

has died and I read closely, searching for something,
evidence perhaps that once these women met.

Oh, Bloomington, Indiana, I always knew you
to be a *thin place* where worlds could overlap;

since they both loved music, maybe these time-twins
found themselves next to each other

at a School of Music concert? Mueller and Brahms
were both born in Hamburg,

so let's say the concert was the *German Requiem,*
where Brahms perhaps gave back to the poet

the city of her childhood that history burned.
Lisel Mueller, tonight I read words you wrote

in the heartland where I was raised, and I'm
up much too early in your nocturnal Germany,

where your poems are like trying on another life,
the way I borrow the coat of my friend, Eoin,

and step out into starry Berlin. Oh, *Knock*
and it shall be opened unto you. So often

I've enjoyed the sound of someone
singing as they passed beneath my window

and now it's me circling the block, offering
my voice to the one night that circles us all.

Monomyth

Start with the known world, which
for me, at this moment, is a bleak
room in Galway where I await my doctor.
Introduce a beautiful stranger
who enters the room with her daughter

and says, *Zoe, be good,*
then disappears behind the covers of *Vogue*
and electric blue nail varnish.
Zoom in on three-year-old, dark-eyed Zoe
who sizes things up and, too short

for the receptionist to notice
as she slips past the desk, pauses
at the room's edge, looks back
at her reading mother and, seeing me,
puts a finger to her lips to command

complicity before vanishing
into the realm where any disease
or suffering might wait for her
but *should* and *good*
at least are vanquished. For a long

minute she explores the moon's dark side,
I glance at the mother who turns
serenely to the next page
and Zoe reappears, her face
serious, radiant and unreadable.

We nod to each other
and then the receptionist
mispronounces my name
and it's my turn to head off
around the corner of the earth.

Night Train to Venice

1

Montepulciano, November 2010

Flawed premise from the start –
an hour to explore in this hill town
before joining Annie
and I mistook Saint Donato,
buried in Venice, for the Donato
who composed madrigals,
also buried in Venice.
Happy error. Stepping onto
Via di San Donato, I sang what I knew
of 'All Ye Who Music Love'.

Singing from the wrong Donato
I headed from the Piazza Grande
down Via Ricci and was stopped
by the sound of sorrow.
In a courtyard of the Palazzo Ricci
a soprano was rehearsing Górecki's
Symphony of Sorrowful Songs.
Late autumn's early darkness.
She stopped, started again, practised
ascending grief's ladder.

Start off singing from a madrigal, return
with words a girl wrote on a wall
of a concentration camp, set to music
by Górecki. I hadn't yet learned
he'd just died, but as I lingered
beneath such sadness, the whole world
might have ended. The music

stopped, I walked on
and the lights in the valley
were candles in a starless church.

Down Via del Paolino to Via di Collazzi,
where last year we rented a room
with a framed print above the bed
of Piero della Francesca's
pregnant Madonna, fitting, since I was
trying to celebrate the first birthday
since my mother's death. I paused
above the valley, recalling
Mother's teaching me
to make memory scrapbooks

then wondered if the Palazzo Ricci
might be connected to *The Memory
Palace of Matteo Ricci,* a book
I half-recalled about a Jesuit
who taught mnemonics
to his Chinese hosts. It doesn't matter
that later I found no link, by then
I'd made an outdoor version of Ricci's
inner palace, linking each street
to the memory of a loved one.

Ricci's memory palace was based
on a Greek poet whose works survive
only in fragments. After Simonides
left a drinking party, the building
collapsed, crushing his family
and friends beyond recognition.

Walking past the tables in his mind,
Simonides recalled where each reveller
had been, helping the living reclaim
what there was to reclaim.

Since then, waking at night, I often
walk this route in my mind, recalling
loved ones, and if I make it back
to Via di San Donato before sleep,
I set off on pilgrimage to Venice,
to Murano and the Church
of San Donato where three huge ribs
hang like upturned crescent moons
beneath the Madonna's feet, proof
that Donato once killed a dragon.

The palace collapses on our friends,
our families. Heartbreak
and then a route through dark streets,
searching for the chapel
of the human heart. Three ribs
levitate in the spinning light.
Dragon or dinosaur. Whale
or dragon. Outside,
the star maze appears
above the shining water roads.

A silent car climbs the steep hill
across the valley. Was the soprano
practising for a concert or offering
her own tribute to Górecki?
I walked on when she finished, linking

hill town streets to friends and family,
but Górecki found a way to remember
the six million dead. He created
a ladder of complete silence.
Then let one voice ascend.

2

Antibes, March 2011

Strange, once again
to be night-journeying, it seems,
towards Venice,
though I was only there
a few hours, forty years ago,
and almost managed
to miss it completely. Only
the impossible bones
in the church of San Donato
made any sense –

Call it the Little Library
of the Road, the way the right book
sometimes waits for you
in a hotel or train compartment.
So F. Scott Fitzgerald
welcomed us to Antibes:
on a shelf in the stairwell, Annie found
a copy of *Tender is the Night*
which she continued reading to me
even after I'd fallen asleep.

My turn to read next night.
Didn't try to go back
where I'd last been awake. Began
where Annie left off, trusting
my dream-self heard
all that I need know, hoping
I recalled the story enough
from reading the book

four decades ago
on a night train to Venice.

Once he said, *Draw your chair up*
close to the edge of the precipice
and I'll tell you a story –
fragments then of Fitzgerald
at the rim of sleep,
like tesserae in a mosaic,
clear glass on both sides
of gold leaf so candlelight
will be more luminous
than the glimmer of narrative itself.

All week our day-selves drove about
looking for where our night-selves
had been at bedtime, partying
with Nicole and Dick Diver.
The village of Tarmes
isn't on the map, but Fitzgerald
set his rose-coloured Villa Diana
five miles from Cannes,
so starting with that landmark
we sought out roads to the precipice.

Four decades ago, Annie praised
Tender is the Night in a letter,
so I took it on the train to Venice.
An Austrian psychiatrist next to me
was travelling to see a French girl
in Murano. He spoke English well
and was charming, a young Dick Diver,

but he criticized Fitzgerald
for glorifying the edge. *Don't
go seeking the abyss. It will find you.*

Those days, I was just trying
not to go mad. My consciousness
had an alarming ability to suddenly
lurch out of my head
so I'd have to hold fast
to whatever was there
until I found my way back
inside the old brainpan. The precipice
for me was the fear of the broken
ladders of the family tree.

Nicole grabbed the wheel,
forcing the car towards the edge,
hitting a tree instead. The children
screamed as she faced Dick
triumphantly: *You were scared
weren't you?* she accused him. *You
wanted to live.* What
could he say, though he didn't.
Yes, fear of death, but also
fear of the crack-up. Precipice fear.

I made it through Fitzgerald
to the Church of San Donato
and his dragon, but returned abruptly
to the station, impatient to get back
to Vienna for Annie's promised letter.

All these years above the sheer
drop and we still read
to each other, waking or asleep.
Do you remember where we stopped
last night? – No, Love. Just keep reading.

II

Memory Train

a lyric essay for Greg and Candy Dawson

When we ask directions to Lynchburg's Riverside Park, we're warned twice against going out on the train trestle and, when I see it, stretching two hundred feet above the James River, I understand the temptation of scaling the fence and following tar-streaked ties above shimmering water. On our side of the river, the tracks vanish into a ravine behind the barrier, and since we never see the rails as we walk home, we guess they must be tunnelling beneath us. Later, I hear the train's horn and can't tell if it's beyond or below or above me. Out there, or somehow in here.

~

I read about the deaths, accidental and otherwise, that have taken place on the trestle, and about the front row seats forced on the engineers, no way to stop the train though they tried, of course, and risked going off the rails. I used to work in a psychiatric hospital where inmates sometimes escaped and lay down in front of trains. In the nineteenth century, asylums were often built outside town, along the rail lines for easy access, so suicide on the tracks was common. I remember riding the train, passing by the hospital, the horn sounding as we neared town.

~

Leaving Lynchburg by train, we suddenly enter the tunnel we'd guessed must exist, and then we burst from the dark onto the trestle, there's light all around us, the train slows so time slows too and we're the ones wobbling across the tracks now. Why is the horn's sound so haunting? It doesn't matter, there are shining islands in the river and nothing but light up here on the high bridge. I'm right here in the moment that stretches out infinitely and, if I could, I would write this whole essay while we're above the James River, stretched between the past and the future. But just like that we've made it to the other side.

~

We've made it to the other side, which is now Orlando, Florida, and the time for the interview has arrived. Before Greg and Candy start taping, we talk a bit, and the first thing I didn't know was that the bullet entered our high school English teacher's heart, not his brain – over the years, I've gotten that detail wrong in a series of poems. When it's time to begin, Greg asks if I'd like coffee and I say, Oh, no, I'm going to need wine. We seem to be firmly here in the present moment, but we are heading back to the ruins of the past, trying to reconstruct what happened almost half a century ago. *Moment,* from the Latin *momentum,* to move. Everything that is right now, the What Is, already in motion, here and then not here. Which leaves us with memories, or fragments of time from which we make our stories.

~

How did you hear about Chuck's death?

I don't know. Maybe a friend called? We were in Massachusetts, on holiday.

~

A train horn sounds as we talk and I pause to listen. Throughout this trip to the States, we've stayed, over and over, in places close to tracks. During our five weeks in

Virginia, I woke so often to those horns that I learned the pattern: two long blasts, a short one, a final long one. I listened with a strange thrill to those wails, then let the long muted roar of wheels on steel lead me back to sleep.

~

You went to his funeral, right? How did you get back to Indiana?

I don't know. Hitchhiked, maybe, or took a bus? I walked to the church from our house, walked that whole bereft town, so I didn't have a car. Is it possible that he was the first dead person I'd ever seen? That wax figure wasn't Chuck. But at least it was permitted that he go into the earth with his Beatles haircut intact.

~

The present is the lyric moment, the kingdom of what is, and as such it is a kingdom we can never possess, since it slips through our hands in an instant.

~

Why did you travel so far to go to his funeral?

Good question. For years I've called Chuck 'my favourite teacher in high school', but some time ago I realised I'd never actually taken a class with him. So what made me travel a thousand miles to that funeral? One reason I started writing poems was to answer such questions. The earliest one about Chuck, written by grief, was never published. It began, 'Somewhere before Bardstown' and laments 'the kindest, the most gentle man'. All my anger was directed at the school board, at the police.

~

When I believed in them, when I was a child, I heard ghosts call outside my bedroom window. Afraid to run to my parents' room, I tried to call for help, but my vocal chords were paralysed. The ghosts came closer and finally a scream escaped my lips. It's only a train, my mother told me. She joined me at the window. No ghosts, no train, just our moonlit-haunted yard and moaning in the distance.

~

I was fifteen, at a party at Jana's house, and Chuck Walls joined us to smoke pot. After that, I'd sometimes drop by his classroom and see what he'd written on the blackboard. Song lyrics as poetry. Surely I remember, *No one dares disturb the sounds of silence.*

~

What clues were left from that party to make Jana's parents read her journal?

~

There is our first realm, the past, which in its truest state is lost to us even if it just happened this morning. So much is forgotten and the rest is in fragments, but we're already at work valuing this, making a story of that, of remembering, which means reinventing, making a moment memorable, making it anything but what it was.

~

My earliest memory: being held in Mother's arms, looking down from a bridge as a train engine enters the roundhouse. It's winter and I snuggle into her coat. I'm not sure I remember anything else before the age of three, so call this the beginning of my train of memory.

~

The first layer of reclamation is easy: check newspaper clippings, verify dates, read that in November 1967, Chuck Walls was suspended for smoking marijuana with students and a criminal investigation began.

~

The second layer depends on memory. Greg has been hosting a virtual class reunion as he and his wife research a book about Chuck's death, and friends I haven't thought of in decades begin confirming (or not) what I thought I knew. But their memories are fallible, too. When I bring up the bus trip from Bloomington to New York City Greg and I took when we were fifteen and the week we spent exploring Manhattan, he doesn't remember it. I describe the trip in detail, but the only thing he thinks he might recall is eating at Mama Leone's. The rest of that unforgettable trip is for the moment irretrievable.

~

We claimed Jana had been hallucinating. Didn't the journal her parents read reveal she'd smoked pot? We all signed affidavits saying we were at the party and Chuck was not, and improbably the superintendent reinstated him, on probation. Others agree that I seem to have been the one who dreamed up this ruse.

~

Chuck's lawyer took the affidavits to the school board and the school board turned them over to the police, so a man named Ed Applegate appeared one evening, a friend of my parents I think, a neighbour on Maxwell Lane, a lawyer or an FBI agent, I'm still trying to figure that out, and he took me up to my parents' room and shut the door. I was in a lot of trouble, I knew that, right? But I could make it all go away. The police didn't want the little guys, they wanted Chicago's mobsters, the ones getting rich sending drugs to our town.

But I wouldn't be a narc. I was scared as hell, but I wouldn't do that.

~

How can the train's horn sound high and low at the same time? Well, it's a chord, five notes, I'd never known that. The Nathan AirChime K5LA, built to resemble the sound of the old steam whistle. I'm surprised to find that I, who am almost phobic about noise, love to be awakened by the horn of a train.

~

Before a hated pep rally, Chuck unlocked the door to the darkroom so we could take refuge and discuss *One Flew Over the Cuckoo's Nest*, yet another book they wouldn't let him teach. Sulfur smell from the developing tanks as we followed his lead, drew connections between Nurse

Ratched and his English department chair. Is it any wonder that Virginia Elkins/Big Nurse kicked me out of my creative writing class that term? I've always said that we had 'creative differences', but now I wonder if Chuck helped hone those artistic disagreements.

Or did art distort things, years ago, some long-forgotten draft of a poem giving Chuck those words? No one else seems to remember those darkroom discussions, so perhaps I made them up, seeking to shed some light on what Chuck meant to us but maybe pushing whatever really happened further into shadow. Well, Ken Kesey would say, 'It's the truth even if it didn't happen'.

~

So much is forgotten and the rest is in ruins. No surprise that Jana writes that, even though she knows it happened, she can't remember smoking pot with Chuck.

~

Last night I got out of bed to try and unpack the spectral sound of the train's horn as it passed. It's a B Major 6th chord, which means exactly what? Say that D-sharp is the note of departure, of escape from a provincial home or of seeking adventure. And the F-sharp sound might be nostalgia, things remembered from a distance. How about G-sharp? The eternal present, the sound at the centre of everything? Then the B chord, floating above the first three chimes, like the future rushing towards us: a note of terror or warning or maybe something thrilling? Finally D-sharp again, but an octave higher, because we can never return to the same place.

~

I didn't know, or else I'd forgotten, that Chuck died a block away from the house where I'd lived as a child. How far does the sound of a gunshot carry? It was an indoor shot, that must have muffled it a bit, so probably most folks went about their business. Until the squad cars arrived.

~

In one early poem, Chuck appeared at Jana's party wearing a Sherlock Holmes hat, with a dope pipe he'd bought in London. My invention, surely.

~

No question that he was cool, but sometimes I think I helped kill him. Sometimes I think if I hadn't lied, hadn't helped him get his job back, he wouldn't have fallen that second, greater time. I keep seeing him draw the key to the darkroom from his Harris Tweed coat pocket with a flourish. Half-smile, half-smirk as he opens the door to red-lit darkness.

~

And the fifteen-year-old boy who did what I refused to do and helped set up his former teacher? If that had been me, how would I have coped after Chuck's suicide?

~

In another poem about the 'death of a favourite teacher', I'd pencilled a timeline of artists on my closet door. We'd learned art by working backwards, starting in the present and leading us past the donors and Madonnas until at last we reached Lascaux and the caves of the ochre deer. The young teacher leaned against the blackboard and seemed to share the gentle grace, the dreaming beauty of those deer. But then I pushed back farther in those caves and found the image of a wild boar, bristling with arrows, fighting for his life and losing.

~

Sometimes my students tell me something like, 'I'll have to wait until he dies before I write about him'. But who is more vulnerable than the dead who cannot defend themselves? Well, he should have thought of that before he pulled the trigger …

~

Grief, and the need to understand what he had meant to us all back then, wrote the first poems. Later, anger helped: where were his boundaries? How could he let his students lie on those affidavits and court such trouble? And after we did, how could he get caught again so soon? How could he leave us?

~

Inside all of us, the train horn we've heard in childhood. It's reverberating deep within, waiting to depart.

~

Summer now, Massachusetts, and an afternoon swim with my sister is interrupted by thunder. After supper, she wants to swim again, but I'm not interested until the lighting turns spectacular and there is no choice. This feels so important: the view across the marshes at high tide towards the end of day, the water dark and the trees dark but the grasses at the edge of the marsh a luminous green, and the white gulls and white herons flying in that golden space between the dark cove and the dark trees, above a green that is like no other green I can name. I want to go to the house for my camera but know the light will change. Just be in the moment, I tell myself. But then it's over and I can only write this down, trying to name what has just happened, trying to say what that light or that green or that golden space must have meant.

~

By this point, have I let the anger go? Can I allow myself to see that young man – only twenty-three – who, whatever his faults, did his best to teach his students in the midst of all that was most wrong and most joyful? I was living on Cape Clear Island off the coast of West Cork when I wrote my most recent poem about Chuck. Our house was high above the Atlantic, that great kingdom of flux that is lined with ruin. It seems somehow fitting to leave the last crucial detail wrong.

NIGHT TRAIN

I wake to the bent harmonica wail of a train, listen
to that childhood echo until I realise I'm on an island, eight miles
from the mainland. The unmistakable roll of countless wheels,

smooth glide of metal over metal, impossible
but passing relentlessly sleep's gate,
so I rise from bed, rush outside to understand.

Dense fog whips in, there's no way to see it, but the locomotive
churns by, just out of sight below the cliffs, until I know
it's the wind bringing close the sound of wheel-like waves.

And the whistle – surely the west wind's distorting
the lighthouse horn. Yes, which is not to say
the train's not out there, hundreds or thousands of cars long,

my wife's mother gazing from the window
into the North Atlantic fog, looking perhaps in my direction
though we can't quite see each other,

and Lynda Hull reciting lines into the smudged glass,
and David Dawson with three shades playing
Beethoven's *Quartet in A minor*, music for the deaf,

and James Merrill, looking up quizzically from his
   portable *OED*,
and – enough. It's cold out here. Back inside
to add coal to the fire. The house rocks in the wind,

hurrying somewhere. I think Chuck Walls
is on that train, still holding his gun in his lap, rubbing
the exit wound at his temple to see if it's started to heal.

III

LITTLE COLLOQUIUM BY THE SEA

The sea is as near as we come to another world.
– Anne Stevenson

I

Because in a former life
I worked twenty years as a nurse
and never saw anyone

nail their exit so perfectly,
last summer, when my father
stopped breathing,

I howled and laughed,
both at once,
a death so gentle:

ninety-one
and living on his own
terms till the end.

And later, seated on a plane
across from a novelist I recognised
from author photos,

I watched his total concentration,
submerged in the creation
of a world

I hope to enter someday, fingers
coming down on the keyboard
almost all at once like

some sort of weather that can dash and lift
and console and break us
with a single word.

II

After a month of conferences,
we arrived home in Ireland
and my wife led me

into the North Atlantic.
How could I know
our hearts wouldn't stop

when we entered those icy
waters? We splashed
the cold onto our arms

and chests before the plunge.
Having survived that
I swim daily now,

late into the fall, preserving
this space to somehow
be with my father, though he

would have been the first
to laugh, and I'm not sure
how I could have explained.

III

Because he learned to love Pinot Grigio late in life,
after his hearing was shot, he called it
Pinot GRATCH-ee-ah,

and I'd try to correct him, *Pinot GREE-gee-o,*
and he'd agree*, Pinot GRATCH-ee-ah,*
and we'd leave it at that,

which was just as well, as today I learned,
in *Wine for Dummies*, it's pronounced
Pinot GREE-joe.

After the rest of us left, my sister found
Dad had stocked enough Pinot Grigio
to make it through the Apocalypse

so she brought bottles to his friends. Perfect,
since Dad loved combining the virtues
of visiting the sick

and giving drink to the thirsty
by smuggling chilled bottles of wine
to friends in the nursing home –

'It cheers them up', he'd say.
It must have cheered my sister too,
talking with his friends,

and when I confessed
that I was wrong all along about the name
she described lingering over a glass

with Dad's Italian friend Giulia
who said, 'I never heard him say
Pinot GRATCH-ee-ah, it sounded

more like *GRAZ-ee-ah*. Sometimes, he could be
almost courtly. *Grazie, molte grazie',*
and Giulia raised her glass to the air.

IV

Approaching the beach, I stopped and watched
as a teenage girl, dignified and dreamlike
in black, approached

the water's edge and, surrounded by family,
did her best to offer a box of ashes
to the sea. More powdery bone

fell on stones than water, but the tide
would gather it all. A man
who must have been her father.

Three boys who could be brothers. And a seal
that appeared a short way out
and gazed at them

until the family left. Finally,
I entered the water,
which was like continuing

the conversation with my father
at the same place we'd left off.
And the seal appeared again, sunlight

on its slick grey dream of a face, round black eyes
looking at me from that world
I could only visit briefly.

V

Our neighbour says I'll be able to swim
all winter since I started in August,
as long as I go in daily.

Wasn't it his father who said he could lift
a three-year-old bull above his head
if he started with a calf

and followed through each day?
Then first thing every morning
didn't he do just that? *And could he*

really lift the bull? Oh, we'll never know,
our neighbour says. My father
strained his back and had to quit.

VI

From a distance I can never bridge
a seal blows air out its nose
then tucks its head into the water

and with a roll its body follows.
Like Elizabeth Bishop
and her seal in 'At the Fishhouses',

I'm becoming a believer
in total immersion.
I swim out to where the seal was

and find myself circled
by islands, snowy mountains,
and the open sea.

Cold water makes sure I know
I am here, now,
never more present in the moment.

VII

Memorising 'At the Fishhouses'
leads me to a photograph of Bishop's
childhood home in Nova Scotia,

then a map locating Great Village,
and I realise that decades ago,
before the toll road was built,

our family must have gone
right past her house
en route to Cape Breton.

I find an online video clip
of someone driving through Great Village,
noting each landmark – *There's*

the one-lane bridge ... that's Wilson's
gas station. Bishop's house
doesn't get a mention,

but I know it from the photo,
right across from Wilson's,
and I'm so absorbed

in Bishop's world that when I get up
to make tea I think at first
I'm in Nova Scotia, in her kitchen,

and have to look about to place myself.
Strange rush of confusion
and contentment,

this total immersion in the there and gone.
Who'd want always to be only
in the present moment?

VIII

Once, wide awake, I entered a dream
that tonight's dream echoes,
and in that earlier vision

it was Easter, it was Crete,
it was radiant and travelling
and friends,

and we happened upon the tiny
Church of the Two Saint Theodores.
I'd never heard of even one

Saint Theodore, but there in the 14th century
was a space for my father and myself
and the door left miraculously

open so I could leave a flame
for both saints, the sky
behind them golden, their horses

in perfect harmony,
and the pair of them in leisurely
conversation about the world's end.

Then the night before my birthday,
the dream came that almost
explained these last few months:

a young glass-blower told me I didn't know
enough colours to grieve fully.
She ran her fingers over

a page in a book until the words glowed,
then rubbed them just enough to heat them
into something new,

the hue of the sea before us, *name it,* she said,
and added the colour to the urn
she spun in the air.

Venice is at war with water, she said,
and Theodore, the first patron saint
of Venice, was a Scorpio, a water sign,

which made him
potentially the enemy, but it was Saint Theodore
who taught the islanders

to make glass in every
colour of the Adriatic. Glass,
the solid that can flow like a dragon.

IX

The ninth of November. We're celebrating
Saint Theodore's Day on Achill Island,
a place from which we can look back

across the bay to our own house,
getting the sea's view
of the world we usually inhabit.

A gale so bad our hostess says
she wouldn't get up on such a day
even to get married.

Trudging against the wind to the beach, I open
the guesthouse gate – surprisingly blue –
like the first gate to the first world.

I lay things out for my return from the waves:
towel at the top of the boat bag,
then shirt and sweater

with sleeves right-side out as there isn't time
to wrestle with them when wind
makes everything billow,

each piece of clothing a sail.
I place a large rock on top of the kit
to keep it from blowing away,

then hurry to the water and find
a nightmare bloom of jellyfish.
Up and down the beach

no entrance,
a possible end to this dialogue if they
keep washing in to shore.

X

It isn't possible to swim every day;
anyway, as Annie likes to say, the perfect
is the enemy of the good.

My father knew a little about perfection,
having played on a high school football team
that not only was undefeated

but never scored upon all season.
Being perfect is wonderful, he said,
but then it's over –

he only mentioned it once.
Better to be lucky, he said,
than perfect.

The jellyfish are called mauve stingers,
though they seem more tan or brown
than pale purple:

they guard the sea like a many-headed monster,
reminding me of the dragon
Saint Theodore slew in an ikon,

so maybe I should find a way into those waves –
no, I don't need to fight that battle.
Then a glimpse of my father,

who had never been in a plane,
but there he is, volunteering
to fly for the army, then piloting

a B-24 up the coast of the Adriatic,
past Venice and on to refineries
outside Vienna: flak was *intense*

and accurate, a thousand howling heads
to navigate through.
I'm a lucky man, my father said,

the morning of his death. Seven decades ago
only half the men in his company
returned from that war.

XI

The first flurries of winter.
In my father's greatcoat
I walk the beach before my swim.

Overnight, large rocks
that resemble meteorites
have been tossed up on the strand,

like reminders of how easily everything
can be rearranged.
I don't know how much longer

I'll keep swimming, I'm just following a feeling,
but the logjam of mauve stingers is gone
so I walk the coat back up to the rocks

and return to swim in the November sea
where wind rips spray from the waves
and makes headlong prisms.

XII

The inventors of joy are often asked
how they thought up such a thing,
and to hear him tell it,

it had something to do with the time clocks
being overworked for weeks,
even something to do with a quarrel,

and she says it came after an illness
and during a time when even the birds
seemed stressed and worried.

Both agree that one morning she proposed
they have a date after lunch,
when the storm would hit,

and everything that morning –
the way the wind started wailing,
the way spume shimmered

as it shawled off breakers,
the sound the cork made as wine appeared
before noon – was foreplay.

And when was there last such a storm?
Hurricane-force gusts, but sunlight, no rain,
a day when everything

raced toward them and shone.
When the house began to tremble,
they were the waves

teased into whirlwinds
and also the point beneath those waves
that moved in circles and held still.

They were the ripples of flame
at the bedspread's edge
and the raised glass, the sunlit Chianti,

and just like that it came to them,
the invention of the flying bicycle
built for two,

wheels within wheels
and then the twelve wings
and then the lift off.

~

No one asks how they came up with the name
for their invention: *Afterglow.*
That one seems

self-evident, but it was the name of the joyful boat
his parents, inventors also,
once dreamed up.

After his mother's death, *Afterglow*
became his father's password for everything.
The children warned him,

You need different codes, you have to
keep changing them,
but he chose to remember

that one word, he carried it with him down the years,
and he died without anyone
stealing the secret name.

~

Who can hold onto paradise? From the beginning
we've messed things up,
made what is good difficult.

And needed to reinvent joy.
Again and again. So the celestial hang glider
needs to be imagined,

and the magic swing set that lets two people leap
from the highest arc and linger
in the air for a beatific moment.

And the bed of quiet, the bed of gentle touching,
the bed where even the next kiss
would be too much.

Dream machines that bring us together
and make possible all those deeds of kindness
we perform in the afterglow.

XIII

Too dark now to see the spring tide's breakers
bludgeon the shore road below our house –
they're surely sundering our lane

for a second time this winter –
so we add turf to the fire, start to read
to each other, but find

we can't compete with the storm's howls
and the stove's answering roar. Still,
there's something companionable,

just writing and reading silently in the same room
while gusts outside reach 160
kilometres per hour. 160, the same

speed the Turkish cab driver sustained last fall
through foggy rain all the way to Munich.
Travelling faster than a hurricane, we

were the unrelenting wind that could upend trees
and bring down power lines, a yowl
through the German countryside

that might at any moment be cut short.
Yet inside that potential destruction
stories unfolded, whose tellings

began on the plane earlier; there was ample time
to share whiskey with seat mates
and talk up there after our landing

in Memmingen was called off and we returned
to the swirling clouds, circling
for an hour till the weather eased.

Finally we descended a second time
and just as the runway reappeared –
the safe Earth a few feet away –

we climbed again abruptly
then flew towards far-off
Friedrichshafen. Audrey,

sitting next to us on the plane, had
to get to Munich to give the keynote speech
at a European Union

health conference, so when we landed
she hired a cab then urged us to join her.
No time for the driver

to look up the conference centre
on global positioning, so he typed
the address with one hand

as we soared down a link road.
Tonight, back in Ireland, the windows
pulse like something living.

It's good to be firmly
on the ground, this house of concrete blocks
is going nowhere,

and the thrumming stillness here
is like being in that cab, or that plane,
a place where strangers could share

a few last words, or speak
whatever most mattered. Audrey
trembled as she told us

how she'd just cleared security in Dublin
when she got a call from Canada
to say her brother Ivan had died.

She'd had to continue towards Munich
to give her speech, and now, because it seemed
impossible we'd get there in time,

our gentle cab driver leaned forward
as if being a few inches closer to the road
would help him see

and get us there faster.
Passing an exit, I realised the road
led to the Alpine foothills

where the novelist W.G. Sebald was born,
and I tried to imagine visiting his village,
fog probably freezing

or turning to snow as we entered Wertach,
but we tore on
instead towards Munich,

the speedometer still at 160,
the highway signs warning
of slippery conditions,

and I remembered how Sebald
died at the wheel.
As if to keep her brother

with her in the car, Audrey was telling us
a story that Ivan told her
that their mother told him,

which felt like the way Sebald's character
Austerlitz
recounted intimacies

several speakers deep,
and there was a fine balance
of terror and camaraderie

as we learned that Audrey
had known our late friend Patrick
on Cape Clear Island. Annie and I

first faced winds of 160 on Cape Clear,
where Paddy said, *Island life is like*
being in a boat together, eight miles

out to sea, and we just have to make sure
we all stay in the boat.
Then Annie told Audrey

how Paddy had died on Cape the same day
she'd had emergency surgery in Boston.
Annie woke to a comforting

hallucination of Fred Astaire and Ginger Rogers
dancing cheek to cheek. She's written
about this – how Astaire

sang at the foot of her bed, *Heaven,*
I'm in heaven – but what connects for me
now is that Astaire's name at birth

was Frederick Austerlitz. So Austerlitz
danced for my wife, who lived, and Paddy
died way too young,

and we'd met his friend Audrey,
we were in this boat together
with her now, we were travelling

faster than some hurricanes
and the cab seemed filled with shades –
Sebald and Paddy

and Audrey's brother Ivan
and the cab driver's wife whose photo
was taped above the dashboard,

the beginning of a story we never got to finish –
and maybe even Fred Astaire.
The distance between life and death

felt very short as we hurtled down the autobahn,
and I recalled how Austerlitz thought
the dead and the living

might occupy the same space,
but those who are already dead
must find the living quite unreal.

And I remembered staring out into the night,
off in the direction of Sebald's birth,
then wondering

if 160 kilometres per hour was the same speed
as the firestorm he described
that rushed through Hamburg

after Allied retaliations, flames reaching
a mile in the air as they sucked
the oxygen from everything.

It will be a long time before I forget
roaring through Germany
as part of that imagined inferno.

I turned the conversation back to Paddy and Ivan.
Destruction and horror are never
very far off, but in the meantime,

there is the chance
to be part of this colloquium
between the living and the dead.

I wish it did not feel so one-sided.
I wish the ones who spoke
were the ones who knew anything.

XIV

Twelfth Night. Six months since Father's death
but a winter storm prevented my swim
until the afternoon wind eased

and I sneaked in for thirty seconds – does that
count? It would have to do
as monsters returned

and blackened the day long before nightfall.
The lights went out, came back, went out,
and we read a little Shakespeare,

raised toasts to Tony and Barbara, the scholar
and playwright who built this cottage
at the edge of the tempest.

~

A wild night, though my dreams
played out a gentle
hide-and-seek: summer,

and we were moving into Castle Cottage,
only it wasn't Annie and me, it was
my parents,

and my mother, so young,
admired then removed the sea rocks
and shells

someone had left on the windowsill,
boxing them carefully
and replacing them

with things she'd brought from the shore,
        making her own window shrine
                which she called *Praise of What Is*.

But when she showed it to my father, she found
        a favourite dappled rock was missing.
                Later, the amber pebble

that glistened on the White Strand was also gone.
        And so the game began:
                what she regarded with pleasure

she brought home and found a place for,
        making patterns
                of dark and coloured forms.

But then, it seemed, some unseen hand
        removed each thing she loved,
                and one by one

her keepsakes disappeared.
        She was at the window when I woke,
                listening to the sea

draw rocks to itself, grind
        them, polish them, return them
                to the strand as if to say:

Here now, something for you to take home,
        something for you to arrange on the sill
                and say that you were here.

~

High tide at 9 in the morning
and we watched from the Breakfast Room
as waves hurled

large rocks onto our road.
What signs and wonders are these
to mark the Feast of the Epiphany?

We're just high enough
that no granite messages
arrive through our windows

like the boulders that appeared
in my mother's home
during the 1938 hurricane.

Until they were removed, she took a sort of pride
in The Hallway Rocks –
who else had anything so wild

indoors? It's fitting that she arrived
in my dreams to help celebrate
the sixth of January

which on Cape Clear Island was called
Women's Christmas, *Nollaig na mBan,*
when men stayed home

to tend house
while women gathered at the pub.
It was Mother

who took me swimming
at the edge of Hurricane Donna
when I was nine, so when the winds

abate a bit, I walk with her in mind
and again do no more
than immerse myself between waves

then start home. There,
in our front garden, is the gunwale
of some boat that's finally

reached shore. Well-weathered, it must have
voyaged for months or years,
so there's nothing to do but rename it

the good ship Viola and welcome it to Illyria,
with a *Hey, ho, the wind and the rain!*
Thank you,

Mother of Storms, for this life
and for preparing me for whatever comes,
For the rain it raineth every day.

XV

At the Boat Inn, in Oughterard, we are shown
not to the usual café
which is being restored (or 'reborn' –

what did our waitress say?) but to a large, airy
dining room where, in a corner,
at an angle to our table,

there's a painting I can't quite see,
but it's the red and gold of the ikon
I dreamed about last night.

A woman hangs her handbag on the back
of a chair, then leaves it to greet the mother
and daughter who sit beneath

my maybe ikon. They form
the sort of triangle
Leonardo might have composed

and I'm 'in the poem' again, everything
shimmering in this place where no one
would steal a purse, and when I order

a pot of tea, no milk, no sugar please,
the waitress walks off singing
Heaven is a place where nothing ever happens.

My good friend, who is usually right,
tells me not to include the word 'poem'
in a poem – *try*

to be less self-referential –
but how else to explain
what's happening?

Is this what hypomania feels like,
everything connecting
faster than I can follow?

While training as a nurse, I thought
I might be suffering
from each and every

psychiatric condition I studied,
briefly fearing I was too much like
the charming but doomed

schizophrenic
I once cared for in Connecticut
who believed his life a movie.

Everyone was given their lines
while he ad libbed his, yet how thankful
he was to be in such a fine film –

even if it would end sadly.
Oh, as Father knew, everything
ends sadly, though I also inherited

his tragic optimism that things might go well
until they can't.
And more and more the everyday

seems charged with a heightened
sense of detail. I can be reading an essay
and look up to see wind

lifting spume from row upon row of waves
and I'll be right back in the poem,
breakers of grief coming in

and gratefulness tossed up and blown
toward the open sea,
so I'll pull on a second sweater

and set off walking.
But if anything can be part of the poem,
surely there's a problem?

Or, maybe, not. Out of the Everything,
luminous images keep emerging
like this morning on the beach

when I met the lady with two lapdogs.
She lives abroad now, but since
her stroke last spring

she's returned to the place where she grew up
to regain her balance, walking on sand.
She's already fallen three times today

but is in good spirits –
when she tosses a ball her dogs leap
into the wind

and are carried a little down-beach,
unable it seems to get enough of
almost flying.

I told her about my father
and the swimming, and she said
we all grieve in our own ways,

for the first year give everyone a pass.
But, I asked, *since all of us*
in any given year

are grieving someone,
don't we ever get to judge
anyone? and she threw the ball

and the terriers named Tutu and Mandela
took to their wings. O excellent dogs
that connect to so many things

I don't know where to turn next.
Forty years ago, after we'd heard
Archbishop Tutu speak,

I asked Annie to marry me.
That was in September
and she didn't answer until October,

so this fall, after Seamus Heaney died,
we took his poem 'Postscript' literally
and drove out west

to the Flaggy Shore on the last day of September
and found things just as he described,
the ocean wild on one side

and the lake to our left *lit*
by the earthed lightning of a flock of swans.
When we told our host, he said

Seamus and Marie took the same room we did
so we'd spent the night as well as the day
inside his poem. On our way home

we stopped for lunch in Kinvara
and got an email saying one of my students
was in a coma.

A few weeks later her next assignment
came in right on time, and the only thing
she'd been aware of during five

unconscious days was a man asking
if she'd like to hear a poem.
The man turned out to be her father,

the poem turned out to be her own
and Heather will write
about that moment herself,

but for me, the conversation was opening, it wasn't
just about my parents, it was as if
we were all being invited to gather

near the abyss and tell our stories.
Once, when I worked in hospitals,
I complained to my friend Linda

that I needed to make more time to write, and she
said, *But Ted, aren't you writing all the time?*
I find I'm writing whether I'm cooking

or hiking or talking with you right now.
I wanted, then, for life
to be a continuous act of attention,

which isn't possible,
although a Trappist monk once taught me
the prayer of the heart, a prayer

that never stops, even when you are sleeping,
a practice that unleashed a lot of joy,
though, like Salinger's character

Franny, I had my mini-crackup and had to stop.
Still, what sweetness, waking and realising
I'd been praying in my sleep

or sometimes I'd be talking
and find a deeper part of me
seemed in conversation with the Real.

I'm not cut out to stay in a poem
          continuously, but my student Anya
                    wrote an essay which ends

with a quote from Leonard Cohen. Cohen works
          five hours a day and, asked
                    what's so difficult about writing,

he said the hard part is
          one has to be *in a state of grace.*
                    Five hours a day living in a poem

might be something to aspire to.
          Our waitress returns, bends to ask
                    if we're okay

and I want to say, *No, not okay, marvellous,*
          as her silver nose ring briefly catches
                    the sun. Even when she

turns away, a bright reflection
          plays on the little spoon
                    I didn't need for black tea.

XVI

Five hours, Leonard Cohen?
Most days I can't find anything
like that sort of time –

something pressing always needs doing –
but I can walk to the strand
and swim in almost any weather.

I can come back to my desk and,
however long, write. Oh, that
sounds assertive, *I can,*

I can, but I fell asleep writing, and now find
my wife has gotten up in the night –
this time she says it's just to read,

this time she's not really worrying
about anything – and I lie on my back
in our bed, arms extended,

filled with a sort of wonder: it's like
those few calm days this summer
when I floated on my back

at Cuainín na Céibhe, eyes closed,
and how I was surprised by the brightest
red dome that formed behind

my eyelids, the sort of opera ceiling
Chagall could only dream of painting.
Seas so still I could have fallen asleep

out there, buoyed beneath the most intense
ruby colour I've ever seen.
In bed, I try to summon that same

hallucinatory hue, and fail –
one must need to be under the open sky
to see it while salt water

hammers sunlight to intensify the glow –
and, lying on my back with a legal pad
and ballpoint, unable

to conjure the molten colour I'd seen, I picture
Dermot Healy, laid out in his coffin
in Ballyconnell, with a fountain pen

sticking up from his pocket. He once read to us
sections from a book-length poem,
then took me walking on fossilised coral

as waves crashed in front of us – *Watch the dog,*
he said, *if the dog makes for home*
move fast or a sleeper wave will take you.

I've entered the North Atlantic almost every day
since returning from my father's deathbed,
immersing myself in the sounds of

land and wind and sea conversing, which is like
sitting in a café, say,
in Slovenia, overhearing

animated talk – I understand and have
no idea what is being said.
I swam, once, as two rays of sunlight

– Jacob's Ladders, we used to call them –
slashed through the clouds
to light up Mayo's coast,

and I wanted my rotator cuff to be up for the swim
across the bay so I could bathe in the midst
of those wonders. The slanting shafts

spotlit the waters well beyond my range,
though I found myself farther out
than I had ever been.

I thought if I floated on my back the lights might
come to me so I waited, out of my depth,
but they remained where they were.

Maybe it's all revelation,
yet the real conversation
seems to be going on above my head.

When my father was in his late eighties,
he found he could no longer
float on his back.

I cradled him once
in Bourne's Cove, supporting his legs,
telling him to breathe in

and hold the air in his lungs,
just as years ago during a hospital field trip
I'd taught an abused child

to trust the sea and lie on his back,
but Dad gave up, frustrated
and confused:

since the age of six he'd known how to float
and now that too was taken.
Life at the edge of the marvellous.

Last winter I watched a charged, dark cloud
sweep away across the bay
towards Mayo –

I wish I'd had a camera
to zoom in at the centre
of that column of energy

where everything inside was starting to swirl.
And on Valentine's Day, Mweelrea
turned white as the storm rushed

towards me, so, for a very short time,
I swam in snow.
For almost a year now,

I've entered the waters beneath that mountain,
and each day Mweelrea is an overflow
of perception, it fills me and is almost

sayable, a slope of sun and moving cloud shadow
that has begun to seem like Cézanne's
Mont Sainte-Victoire, a peak

to be studied daily and brought inside.
Some mornings that far shore has glimmered
like paradise, but in the end

I must have gone back home and paid my bills
or written words that, even if I could
find that state of grace,

cannot bring my parents back.
Then the Rembrandt House
in Amsterdam comes to mind,

where, in five successive
etchings made from one copper plate, the artist
scraped away

most of the figures on Calvary,
making the scene darker and simpler, until He
who said, *I am the Light of the World,*

is crucified in a hail of darkness.
It was about the sixth hour
and there was a darkness

over all the earth. The night passes, I hear
Annie on the stairs heading down
to make coffee. It is time to join her

in the Breakfast Room. We'll eat porridge
with Greek yogurt, berries and pecans,
we'll gaze out at Mweelrea.

Two or three hours I've been in the poem
and I worry what will happen
if I ever finish the Little Colloquium.

Wasn't Cézanne
granted the grace to paint
his mountain till the end?

XVII

Variations on *The Simple Truth*

Insomnia again, because tests suggest
the serene sleep aid I've taken for years
might invite dementia.

Which is why I was up before dawn
to look through our window and see
what appeared to be distinct

tongues of flame
rising from our overgrown hillock.
I thought a chimney spark

had ignited a grass fire,
but as I crossed the room to check,
I passed between

the stove and window
and saw the flames had only been reflections
in the glass pane.

Still, take one step to the left
and the whole peninsula
looked at risk from windblown fire.

Staring at the burning grass,
I tried to correct my vision
but the blaze resisted being dismissed.

~

Next morning, in predawn light,
the fire on the knoll appeared
to materialise again, and I entered

that liminal realm where this world
    and the imagined one
        ignited in one burst.

The dim room gathered about me
    but I was wide awake, gusts
        agitated the tall grasses, and flames

rippled like scripture
    I could almost decipher.
        Morning after morning,

the burning hummock awaited,
    so that fairy fire
        seemed scientifically provable,

the gift of quitting Benadryl,
    and I would wake up early
        and write by the light of that blaze.

~

Hard to leave those Connemara mornings
    and fly to the States to teach.
        We beat a storm to Massachusetts

and that first night
    in the university guesthouse,
        I woke and watched the blizzard

from our window, wondering as lights
    flicked on, swirled about and vanished,
        as if motion detectors

were reporting the movements
of snow dervishes
that gusted from drifts the nor'easter

kept manufacturing. I seemed to be
working night shift too, already
breaking my new rule against

checking the Net before breakfast,
which is how I learned
of Philip Levine's death.

Levine, who never broke faith
with the fourteen-year-old self
who toiled for Chevy. Surrounded

by men who swore or sang
into the thunderous air,
he must have felt screened by the din

so he could recite poems,
a lot of communication
going on with nothing, no one to hear.

Wind assaulted our dormers.
Out there in the fitful cold,
something

was going on
that I didn't understand
and it kept triggering the light.

~

Ever since Adam, how do we resist
the temptation of instant
knowledge? True, that morning

without the Web I wouldn't have known
that Phil Levine had died
and yet those shining screens

seem to snag each moment of time
and keep my mind from settling anywhere.
I have known all this before –

a fire that was not a fire, a motion that was
not only a ghost. Swirls from the snowdrifts
that announced another wanderer.

~

At the airport, the short-term garage
brought back a memory
of my father's car

abandoned across multiple parking spaces,
driver's door left open,
key still in the ignition,

after the television loop
that was supposed to be breaking
news put him to sleep

and he woke to find we'd landed in Indianapolis.
Ninety, proud and not wanting us
to worry, he improved

on the speed limit
all the way from Bloomington,
hastened to the arrivals hall

then couldn't recall
where he had parked.
When we finally found

his sedan, we sensed
how disaster might be presaged
by a car's dizzy angle.

~

When did my life become
one forward plunge
through workdays that lasted

almost until bed and required
a gentle dart so I could find
a green place to lie down inside?

Oh farewell to Benadryl,
how I missed you,
morning's dry mouth and all,

but I wouldn't court dementia.
Instead, I got up and read how Phil Levine
used to begin most days

in a high room between two rivers
looking for words to *welcome*
morning across the junked roof tops.

~

February 2012, Dad's car abandoned
across three parking spaces, an image
I'm only able to confirm now

because my journal is digital,
and there I find this detail: soon after
he picked us up it was halftime,

Indiana led first-place Michigan,
but when he tried to cross his fingers
for good luck, arthritis

wouldn't let his hand make that dance.
And the car at an angle across three
parking spots –

is that even possible? Yes,
for all of us, of course,
such a car exists,

and it takes up that much space,
it takes up everything
we can't understand.

~

Until that car arrives, how then
shall we live? I thought of Phil Levine
describing his mentor

John Berryman
who held up a copy
of the *New York Times*,

the closest thing to the Internet
          in those days, and told the class
                    the sum of what you could learn

in the papers: one political party
          will hurt us, then the other one will.
                    Berryman thought we needed story,

needed narrative to bring us to the place
          of transcendent song. John Keats
                    will be ours as long as language lasts.

~

Time glows then ignites.
          We visited a friend who has begun
                    losing names and memories;

he handled that knowledge with the utmost
          grace, yet admitted to feeling bereft,
                    said there's a different pitch

when he cries, as if the sobbing comes
          from somewhere deeper
                    than he's ever known.

Still, there he was, tending the wood fire
          as I entered the kitchen, coaxing
                    scrolls of flame to rise.

Our wives joined us, the four of us
          warmed ourselves
                    at the fire Doug built,

sparks flew against the stove's glass door
        and we ate sesame seed bagels
                and honey,

things so simple and true
        that Levine would have turned
                to the reader and asked

Can you taste
        what I'm saying?
                No matter how early one gets up

there are things we have no words for,
        things as basic as a pinch of salt.
                And we live on them.

~

Woke from a good sleep and found
        we were home at last in Connemara.
                Wind quickened

our neighbour's trees,
        arrived at our gate
                then a moment later

surrounded our cottage, the sound
        all about me. And yes,
                when I built

on the remains of last night's fire,
        even in that downpour
                there was a small

curtain of flame
        out there in the unmown grass.
                Then the rain stopped telling

its endless story
        and moved on, leaving this silence.
                I added more turf, tended

the two fires, the vortex in the stove
        and our small hill's bright flames
                that cannot be, but are.

XVIII

My arms lead the way through summer water,
past the platform the clam harvesters set up,
beyond the floats and traps.

I'm feathering through an absence of waves –
the cove my mother swam in
as a child –

and the opposite shore
is watery light flickering on reeds
and meadows,

morning reflected
into moving oak leaves
and an osprey's shrill call

as it glides in
to its nest.
Jahrzeit, and we've gathered

to join Father's ashes
with Mother's
and to open

boxes with some scrapbooks
we have never seen – the war years
(which were never

to be spoken of) and numbered
love letters that leave us
wondering where the others

are (the girl who will become
my mother writes to her own mother
about this young pilot

with *Ronald Colman eyes –*
I don't really care if other people
don't approve).

Almost seven decades
of memories and clues to sort through
and then, towards the end,

my mother's blindness,
and the words she wrote
for herself on black paper

with a white marker
and a magnifying glass, her credo
which urged her

to learn to love
to improve discipline
to improve patience (pray

while you wait).
So many friends just now
trying to be patient

until they hear about their biopsies, job interviews
and the births of grandchildren:
what better way

to learn to pray
than this time we spend
in our various waiting rooms?

I didn't know
I'd keep swimming all year
or that I wouldn't stop

when the year ended.
And now, preparing to fly back home
to Ireland,

I start Michael Cunningham's new novel,
The Snow Queen.
It's the book he was writing

on the plane last summer,
and it begins,
A celestial light

appeared to Barrett Meeks
in the sky over Central Park ...
Signs and wonders!

Once, over Greenland, I woke
to find the Northern Lights
spiralling far above and beyond

the wing of our plane, so now
I ask my wife for the window seat
and look out into the night

as often as I can. Oh, the darkness
has never been larger.
Our plane has dimmed its lights

and hurtles into blackness.
Adam Zagajewski says,
Swimming is like a prayer:

palms join and part,
join and part,
almost without end.

It's the *almost* that makes prayer
human. *Without end*
touches the night skies.

XIX

Father, this morning I walk to the beach
wearing your coat like another skin.
I remember you asking, *Where's Dougie?*

and we'd point to your shoulders, *You're*
carrying him! and you'd crane
your head to the skies and say, *I don't see*

anyone. Where's Dougie?
and we'd shriek with laughter. A game
played all the way to the sea

where you'd lower my brother to the sand
and ask, *Where were you?* and he'd say
On your shoulders, and you'd look

at both shoulders and say, *There's no one*
there. You're on the beach!
While the waves

come in and withdraw, the gentle dispute
between generations continues,
You're there, You're not there.

ACKNOWLEDGEMENTS

Thanks to the editors of *Cyphers, Even the Daybreak: 35 Years of Salmon Poetry, Mud Season Review, Numéro Cinq, The SHOp, Solstice Online, The Stinging Fly, The Stonecoast Review* and *Stone House,* where some of these poems appeared, often in earlier versions.

'Night Train' first appeared in *Cape Clear: New and Selected Poems* (Salmon, 2002).

Special thanks to Betsy Sholl, Joan Newmann and Kate Newmann who read and commented on these poems and offered their invaluable thoughts on them.

And heartfelt thanks to Annie Deppe, insightful first reader and the bringer of gladness and delight.

ABOUT THE AUTHOR

Theodore Deppe is the author of *Children of the Air* and *The Wanderer King* (Alice James Books, 1990 and 1996); *Cape Clear: New and Selected Poems* (Salmon, 2002); *Orpheus on the Red Line* (Tupelo, 2009); and *Beautiful Wheel* (Arlen House, 2014).

He holds a Master of Fine Arts degree from Vermont College. A recipient of two grants from the National Endowment for the Arts and a Pushcart Prize, he has been writer-in-residence at the James Merrill House in Stonington, Connecticut, and at Phillips Academy in Andover, Massachusetts.

Ted has taught creative writing in graduate programmes in the US, Ireland and England. He is on the faculty of the Stonecoast Master in Fine Arts programme and he directs Stonecoast in Ireland, which brings graduate students from the University of Southern Maine to study in Ireland.

He worked as a registered nurse for twenty years while teaching poetry and fiction classes. Since 2000, he and his wife, poet Annie Deppe, have, for the most part, made their home on the west coast of Ireland. They presently live in Connemara. He is a dual citizen of the US and Ireland.